Boulevard

of

Dreams

Boulevard of Dreams

A Pictorial History of El Portal, Biscayne Park, Miami Shores and North Miami

Seth H. Bramson

Charleston   London

History
PRESS

Published by The History Press
Charleston, SC 29403
www.historypress.net

Cover Image: Pueblo Feliz was one of the first entertainment venues in Biscayne Country and was built at approximately Northeast 16*th* Avenue and 123*rd* Street, although the view shown makes it look much larger than it actually was. Terribly damaged in the September 1926 hurricane, a fire some months later would level what had been planned to be the center of social activities in the area and the site would remain vacant for many years thereafter. *Courtesy of Seth H. Bramson.*

First published 2007

Manufactured in the United Kingdom

ISBN 978.1.59629.274.1

Library of Congress Cataloging-in-Publication Data

Bramson, Seth, 1944-
   Boulevard of dreams : a pictorial history of El Portal, Biscayne Park, Miami Shores, and North Miami
/ Seth H. Bramson.
       p. cm.
   ISBN 978-1-59629-274-1 (alk. paper)
1. Miami Region (Fla.)--History, Local. 2. El Portal (Fla.)--History. 3. Biscayne Park (Fla.)--History. 4.
Miami Shores (Fla.)--History. 5. North Miami (Fla.)--History. 6. Miami Region (Fla.)--History, Local-
-Pictorial works. 7. El Portal (Fla.)--History--Pictorial works. 8. Biscayne Park (Fla.)--History--Pictorial
works. 9. Miami Shores (Fla.)--History--Pictorial works. 10. North Miami (Fla.)--History--Pictorial works.
I. Title.
   F319.M6B73 2007
   975.9'38--dc22
                                        2007011637

Notice: The information in this book is true and complete to the best of our knowledge. It is offered without guarantee on the part of the author or The History Press. The author and The History Press disclaim all liability in connection with the use of this book.

This incredible view was taken from above Biscayne Boulevard (the four-lane road directly below the camera) at Northeast 107th Street. Clifford's Restaurant, a longtime northeast Dade favorite, is in the building at left, with the china store and the alligator goods store in the large building on Biscayne immediately in front of the camera. The motel with the pool at right is the Apache, directly behind which are the buildings of Miami Military Academy. In the late 1970s, the Apache and Miami Military would become history, to be replaced by the Towers of Quayside.

When one fights bigotry and anti-Semitism, one finds that some people will stand with him or her to do right while others—the little minds—will support what is evil. When the battle against that vile bigotry reared its ugly head in Miami Shores while I was general manager of Miami Shores Country Club, several people (unfortunately, too few) stood up for what was right and honorable and ethical, and to them—including the two council members who voted to fire a village manager who rightfully should have been in Podunk, Nebraska, Yokeltown, Iowa, or anywhere but here—this book, with gratitude and admiration, is dedicated.

Contents

Acknowledgements

In writing a book such as this—the first pictorial history of the four communities in primarily northeast Miami-Dade County immediately north of the City of Miami—it was a pleasure to deal with a large number of people and entities who enthusiastically supported our efforts, and I gratefully acknowledge the following:

Warren Bittner, Esq., a great historian in his own right; Lou Soli, of the Miami Shores Chamber of Commerce, who was so very helpful; Bernard "Buddy" Grossman, one of Miami Beach High's greatest scholar-athletes, who suggested the title of this book; Connie Scott Manley, of Manley's Jewelers, who furnished the wonderful photo of herself working in Publix; Mary Robbins, who kindly loaned the marvelous swimsuit photograph; Dave Cohen, from Bagels & Co. on Biscayne Boulevard, who loaned us several photos, including one of that eatery; Jason Walker, village manager and Jannie Richardson, city hall office manager—both of the Village of El Portal—for their time and patience; Robert J. Stobs, of Stobs Brothers Construction Co. in Miami Shores, who went through hundreds of photos with me and loaned a good few that appear herein; Stephanie and Tobie Ansin of the PlayGround Theater in Miami Shores who so graciously encouraged me and loaned several photos; Patrick Duffy, of Duffy Realty in Miami Shores, who was his usual warm and unbelievably helpful self; Dawn Wellman of Beachfront Realty, who most kindly allowed us to use several of her fine photos of El Portal; Richard "Dick" Asker, retired Miami Shores police department captain, who furnished the great MSPD photos; the Board, Director Elizabeth Esper and Maria Temkin of the Miami Shores Brockway Memorial Library, who were so unstintingly helpful and gracious; the mayor and commission, interim Village Manager Frank Spence, Code Enforcement Officer Sira Ramos and Chief Mitchell Glansberg of the Village of Biscayne Park, all of whom bent over backward to help; our friends and fellow members of the Miami Memorabilia Collectors Club; and, of course, Jackie Biggane, Blair Connor, Penny and Bill Valentine, North Miami Councilman Scott Galvin and all of the rest of the wonderful membership of the Greater North Miami Historical Society, which has done so much to preserve the history of the entire area covered by this book. My dear bride (of more than thirty years), Myrna, whose unending patience with a husband who covered the dining room table with stuff for many weeks while preparing this book can not go unmentioned, and to the numerous others who shared their thoughts and memories, my deep and sincere appreciation is warmly expressed.

Unless otherwise credited, all photographs are from the collection of the author.

Introduction

*W*hat an incredible story! And even more incredible is the fact that the story of what the late Thelma Peters referred to—and titled her 1981 book—as *Biscayne Country* may have begun as early as 1535. The story includes romance, intrigue, political infighting and, well, all the things that are going on in the four communities today, as well as in the rest of Miami-Dade County, which Colorado Congressman Tancredo once called "a third world country!"

While that "rest of Miami-Dade County" may or may not be "a third world country," the four municipalities in this volume are pretty stable—other than a virulent anti-Semite serving as village manager in Miami Shores in the late 1980s; a North Miami mayor declaring in 2003 that black police applicants should not have to learn to swim as part of their police academy training because their ancestors came across the water in chains and were never given the opportunity to swim; a North Miami police chief suing her city in 2007; residents of Biscayne Park being engaged in highly charged and rather raucous political issues and "debate" within that lovely community, and El Portal, for the most part, being pretty much at ease—and all seem to get along pretty well.

Names that are familiar to all of south Florida are or were intertwined with the four communities, including such legendaries as Julia Tuttle; her father and mother, Ephraim and Frances Sturtevant; William Wagner; William Henry Gleason; William Hurst; Arthur M. Griffing; Confederate General John B. Gordon; J.T. Gratigny; T.V. Moore; Hugh Anderson; Ellen Spears Harris and Emrys Harris; Frank O. Pruitt; Roy Hawkins; M.R. Harrison; and others who are part of the mosaic that makes up the Boulevard of Dreams.

Their stories are and will forever be entwined with the entities that they built or helped to build. One of them, Biscayne, the predecessor of today's Miami Shores, served as Dade County seat from 1870 to 1880. Jupiter, in today's Palm Beach County, had a good few more than the one hundred or so people then living in the southern part of the county (which ran from Indian Key in the middle of the Florida Keys to just north of Jupiter, and from which half of Monroe County and all of both Palm Beach and Broward Counties were carved) and was able to outvote southern Dade. The county seat moved "up there" until the 1890 election enabled southern Dade to retake the honor and have the county seat moved back to the region around the shores of Biscayne Bay, where it would permanently remain.

The first settlers were essentially subsistence farmers, but eventually Little River (outside the purview of this edition), Biscayne and Arch Creek would become relatively major farming areas, producing truck (produce), citrus and coontie (pronounced "coon-tea," not "coon-tie"), which is the starch plant that if eaten or ingested prior to proper cleaning and milling could be highly toxic and, in some cases, fatal.

The Military Trail—commemorated by today's Biscayne Boulevard, Arch Creek Historic Trail, Northeast 12th Avenue and East Dixie Highway in Miami—was the main avenue of commerce other than the railroad. To denote the importance of the communities, the Florida East Coast Railway established depots at both Arch Creek, just north of today's Northeast 125th Street and Biscayne at approximately Northeast 103rd Street, which would be on today's Miami Shores Country Club grounds but was then a through street known as Biscayne Road.

The region grew slowly and much of the early story of the area is marvelously recounted by the late Dr. Thelma Peters, who grew up in Biscayne country and would for many years teach history at Miami Edison High School. Dr. Peters's book covers the years 1870 to 1926, and though there have been articles and pamphlets published, nothing up to this point has told the complete up-to-date story of the four communities and the unincorporated area between Miami Shores and Biscayne Park and which is also east of Biscayne Park and north of Miami Shores from Northeast 105th Street to the southern city limits of North Miami at Northeast 121st Street.

It is a marvelous and incredible tale and the reader is invited to sit back, relax and enjoy reading about an often overlooked piece and part of the history of Miami-Dade County—an area that, in many ways came about because of a Boulevard of Dreams.

One

El Portal

*E*l Portal, which borders Miami to its east and south, the county to the west and Miami Shores to the north is, with the exception of a business block on Biscayne Boulevard and several offices on Northeast 2nd Avenue, a lovely community of, almost without exception, well-maintained middle-class homes.

The smallest of the four municipalities in this tome, El Portal is bounded on the north by Northeast 91st Street, on the south by the Little River, on the east by Parker Drive and on the west by Northwest 5th Avenue. A prominent feature of the community is the Tequesta burial mound on Northeast 85th Street between Northeast 4th and 5th Avenues, which is a memorial to the Native American tribe that inhabited much of southeast Florida prior to the arrival of the Seminoles and Miccosukee.

While it has been suggested that the location of the Miami Circle just south of the Miami River marks the location of the Tequesta capital, the actual location may have been approximately five to six miles north in today's El Portal, focused on the Tequesta burial mound mentioned above. Some historians have noted that the El Portal area was the oldest nonpermanent European settlement in the New World. Scholars have traced the location as having been the the homesite of a small group of settlers from Spain as early as 1535, some thirty years before St. Augustine was settled (although it was the latter community that became the oldest permanent town in today's United States).

Interestingly, El Portal was originally laid out by one Lee T. Cooper of Dayton, Ohio. Cooper was a pharmacist by title, but his main business was the manufacture of a substance today long-forgotten called Tanlac, along with other proprietary medicines. Sometime in 1917 or '18, Cooper hired a friend from Dayton, Fred Boyer (whose actual vocation was that of a barber) to scout the land and report back to him. Along with what would become part of Miami Shores, Cooper bought much of today's El Portal for as little as twenty-five dollars per acre. (In comparison, the first owners of what would become Ocean Beach and then Miami Beach, Henry Lum and his son, Charles, purchased most of that large sandbar for seventy-five cents an acre!)

It was Cooper who, upon purchasing the 135 acres between a subdivision called Bayview Estates and the Little River section of Miami, would christen his new holding "El Portal," the gateway. As with the other three communities in this volume, El Portal's modern history is nothing short of fascinating: with only a few people living in the community south of what was already known as Miami Shores (but which had not yet formally adopted that name as an incorporated entity), the City of Miami, which had already swallowed up the incorporated municipality of Coconut Grove and had taken over Buena Vista and Lemon City, annexed the area north of its previous boundaries to Northeast 121st Street, including El Portal, in 1925.

While the great Miami boom of the 1920s was in progress, Miami had no problem handling municipal services in its expanded area, but with the bust that occurred following the cataclysmic events of 1926, Miami could no longer afford to provide services north of Northeast 87th Street and sometime in 1931 gave up its claim to the entire area, including all of the property north to Northeast 121st Street.

In 1937 El Portal was incorporated and for some years two wooden gates stood as a gateway to the village. Although only about twenty-five families lived in El Portal at the time of incorporation, the city fathers foresaw the city as a bedroom community for Miami, which, even in the Depression, grew as tourists continued to pour in to the area, many of them staying in the cabins and tourist camps along Biscayne Boulevard adjacent to and east and north of El Portal.

Growth continued through the remainder of the twentieth century and in 2002 the first village manager was appointed to oversee the day-to-day operation of the community. In 2006 Jason Walker, formerly with the City of Miami, was appointed to the manager's position. Walker is well liked by both employees and residents of a village that prides itself both on its diversity and the fact that, since its founding, it has been a bird sanctuary.

The village's citizens are active on civic boards and in local organizations and participate vigorously in village affairs. El Portal—the gateway—celebrates its seventieth year in 2007 and is looking forward to a bright and prosperous future.

Stobs Brothers Construction Co. has been a part of the communities that are tied to the Boulevard of Dreams since the 1930s and one of their fine local projects was the design and construction of the El Portal Village Hall. This view, from a Stobs-issued booklet, provides information about the building and its facilities. *Courtesy Stobs Brothers Construction Co.*

Illustrating the warmth and hominess of El Portal is the house at 8733 North Miami Avenue. *Courtesy Dawn Wellman, Beachfront Realty.*

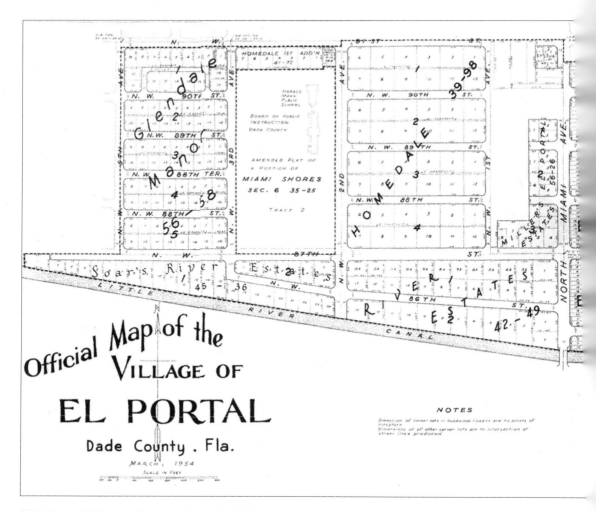

This March 1954 map illustrates the entire Village of El Portal, including the interesting proruption in the southwest corner. It also contains the several blocks on the west side of the village that include Horace Mann Middle School, for many years a feeder school to Miami Edison High School, attended by the majority of students who lived in El Portal and Miami Shores. On the southeast, the business blocks east of the FEC Railway tracks bordering on Biscayne Boulevard are clearly shown. *Courtesy Village of El Portal.*

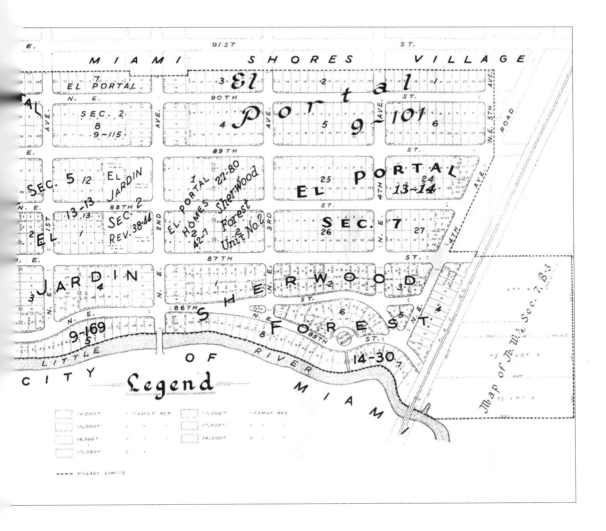

157 Northeast 86th Street is set off by its unique red awnings. *Courtesy Dawn Wellman, Beachfront Realty.*

8670 Northeast 1st Avenue has interesting window treatment arrangements. *Courtesy Dawn Wellman, Beachfront Realty.*

The bungalow at 97 Northeast 87th Street fits in delightfully with the neighborhood. *Courtesy Dawn Wellman, Beachfront Realty.*

The Florida-style screen door at 476 Northeast 87th Street is today a unique and unusual feature of south Florida's homes. *Courtesy Dawn Wellman, Beachfront Realty.*

465 Northwest 88th Terrace is a spacious four-bedroom, two-bath dwelling. *Courtesy Dawn Wellman, Beachfront Realty.*

The beautiful hibiscus in the front sets off the attractiveness of 465 Northeast 89th Street. *Courtesy Dawn Wellman, Beachfront Realty.*

114 Northwest 89th Street was recently remodeled when this photograph was taken, showing the interesting solar-heating apparatus on the roof, right rear. *Courtesy Dawn Wellman, Beachfront Realty.*

Although appearing to be of modest size, this lovely home at 132 Northwest 89th Street sits on a huge lot with room for a good-sized pool. *Courtesy Dawn Wellman, Beachfront Realty.*

For many years Rader United Methodist Church anchored the entire block between Northeast 87th and Northeast 88th Streets on Northeast 2nd Avenue. Although the address was 215 Northeast 87th Street, the church fronted Second Avenue. In early 2007, with declining membership, the congregation elected to merge with another Methodist church, and the building was sold to the Archdiocese of Miami to be converted to a convent and for other uses. *Courtesy Patrick Duffy, Duffy Realty.*

Regretfully, ardent sleuthing could not determine the names of the men in this circa 1956–57 photograph, taken at the El Portal Village Hall and Police Station, but it is abundantly clear that these three men are serving the village honorably and proudly. *Courtesy Village of El Portal.*

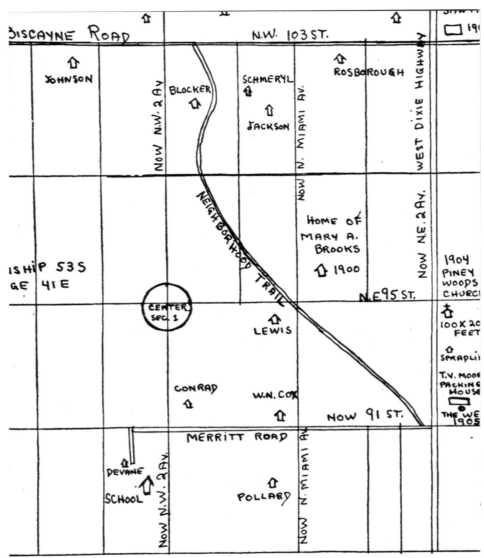

DRAWN BY MELVIN S. MISHLER
WHO HOMESTEADED 80 ACRES IN 1900
(AREA NOW KNOWN AS NW. 10AV. AND 111 ST.)
VERIFIED BY W.N.COX - RESIDENT SINCE 1907
. MARCH 24, 1953

This map was drawn by Melvin S. Mishler, who, as is noted on the image, homesteaded eighty acres in 1900. Happily for us, this map shows the territory from Biscayne Road—Northwest and Northeast 103rd Streets—to Northeast 87th Street (now the south boundary of Miami Shores at Biscayne Boulevard and within today's El Portal) and from west of today's Northwest 2nd Avenue to just east of Northeast 2nd Avenue. The Moore packinghouse is at Merritt Road (today's 91st Street) and West Dixie Highway, while the rectangle showing the location of the Hurst packinghouse is barely visible at top right.

Two

From Biscayne to the Shoreland Company

William Henry Gleason and William Henry Hunt were two incredible rascals of nineteenth-century south Florida politics. "Scalawags" might be a good term for them, although they did much good for the area. In the 1878 Tax Collections Book for Dade County (the oldest piece of marked Miami memorabilia known to exist, now in the author's collection), both are shown as having paid their taxes that year.

Upon moving from the region around the banks of the Miami River to a point about eight miles farther north, Gleason and Hunt named the area "Biscayne." Later other parts of the region would bear the "Biscayne" prefix, followed by surnames such as Heights, Park, Garden and Canal. The Florida East Coast Railway station at what was Biscayne Road, then Northeast 103rd Street and, later, the country club golf course were all named Biscayne.

Hunt and Gleason began to grow coconuts and other agricultural products, but Francis Sturtevant, mother of Julia Tuttle, opined that "South Florida was much better suited to tourism than to agriculture," which, of course, would portend the long-term future of much of the county. Julia Tuttle, identified almost entirely with the lower portion of what would become Miami, also would become—along with her husband, Frederick—a landowner in the Biscayne region.

Eventually, in 1893, a man named Edward Clinton Barnott would receive a homestead patent, and would take over the operation of the Biscayne to Key West mail boat (note that this was *not* Miami) contract from Gleason. Soon after Barnott's death, Mrs. Barnott—Mary—would marry her neighbor, John H. Peden, and it is from the Peden and Barnott families that much of the remainder of the history of the area, leading eventually to the formation of the Shoreland Company, would evolve.

As previously noted, Dr. Peters's *Biscayne Country* provides an almost unlimited resource for those studying the early history of what would in 1932 become Miami Shores. As a matter of brevity, we must move forward to 1904, when A.B. Hurst opened a starch factory and sawmill at what is now Northeast 2nd Avenue and 103rd Street.

A year later, Miami furniture dealer T.V. Moore founded the Biscayne Fruit Company and began planting citrus on a large scale, then built a packinghouse to handle the production. As noted in the previous chapter, Lee T. Cooper came into the picture shortly thereafter and began buying much of Moore's acreage. Eventually, Cooper would own 2,500 acres, much of it comprising today's Miami Shores. By 1923, just before the great Florida boom, he had platted 127 acres.

It was at that point that Tennessean Hugh Anderson would cast his considerable shadow over the area. Anderson and his associates had made a fortune after purchasing the Collins Bridge from Carl Fisher and building the Venetian Causeway and the islands which the causeway would cross. Anderson, with partners Roy C. Wright, J.B. Jeffries and his cousin, Mrs. Ellen S. Harris, would found and form the Miami Shores and Shoreland Companies. Anderson believed that, with the Florida boom notching up almost daily, he and his partners could emulate Carl Fisher (Miami Beach) and George Merrick (Coral Gables) and turn Miami Shores into "America's Mediterranean."

Among the marvelous and incredible Shoreland Company projects was the creation of Miami Shores Island (today known as Indian Creek Village), with plans in the works for a Grand Concourse and Miami Shores Causeway to connect the island to the mainland along with a mid-bay causeway, which would have extended from the Venetian Causeway to Miami Shores Island.

By 1926 the Shoreland Company's land sales were in the tens of millions of dollars and everything looked gloriously rosy—until the events of 1926, which would prove to be the beginning of the end, not just for Anderson and his associates but also for Greater Miami as the great Florida boom of the 1920s became—with the sinking of the Prinz Valdemar at the mouth of the turning basin of Miami's harbor, the FEC's having to embargo itself due to the enormous amount of traffic with no room for incoming freight cars, and the September 17–18 hurricane—the terrible "bust," which would be the harbinger of the Great Depression that would begin in 1929.

Charles Atkinson is another of the almost forgotten pioneer names of the Biscayne country. Atkinson's sawmill was on Biscayne Road, west of Truman's Corner, which was near or at today's Northeast 2nd Avenue. Left to right in this photograph are Mrs. Atkinson, Clyde, Effie, Mr. Atkinson and Robert Earl. *Courtesy Brockway Memorial Library, Miami Shores.*

Pioneer Sam Mishler is driving the then-new truck that made it much easier to bring their main cash crop—at the time, pineapples—to the Biscayne depot. The Mishler logo was an "M" in a triangle with three words—"Smooth Cayenne Pineapples"—on each side of the triangle. *Courtesy Brockway Memorial Library, Miami Shores.*

This picture, which has never appeared before in any publication, is one of the rarest of the Biscayne photographs known. Looking north across the prairie, only scrub palmettos (in foreground) and the pines that were harvested for the sawmills are visible. Taken circa 1914, the photographer is, regretfully, unknown.

The Mishler homestead and sawmill was truly a place of pristine pioneer beauty, shown in the photograph sometime before 1918. *Courtesy Brockway Memorial Library, Miami Shores.*

The Hurst sawmill and starch factory was, as previously noted, on Biscayne Road, just east of Dixie Highway, today's Northeast 2nd Avenue. It is believed that the man at left with his leg on the large crosstie is Albert Baxter Hurst. The ties were being cut to FEC Railway specifications for use on the legendary Key West extension, which was built between 1904 and 1912. *Courtesy Brockway Memorial Library, Miami Shores.*

Above: Hurst was a major promoter. His show wagon participated in most of the pre–Orange Bowl Palm Fest parades as well as the earlier Parade Day events in Miami. Here, the motor-driven truck-float carries members of the family along with his chef, standing center. The sign on the float indicates not only that Hurst produced Florida Arrow Root Starch from the coontie plant but that his sales office was in Little River. It is believed that this photograph was taken in front of the old (pre-1925) Dade County Courthouse on 12th—now Flagler—Street. *Courtesy Brockway Memorial Library, Miami Shores.*

Right: The Florida East Coast Railway was the builder and remains today the backbone and freight lifeline of Florida's east coast. Coming down the east coast, the railroad reached the Biscayne settlement some weeks before arriving at its Miami terminus on April 15, 1896. Photographs of the Biscayne depot, destroyed by the September 17–18, 1926 hurricane are extremely rare and we are fortunate to have this image, even though from a much used copy negative, of a passenger train slowing for the Biscayne stop, circa 1915.

Florida East Coast 4-4-2 wheel arrangement steam locomotive 61 was built by Schenectady Locomotive Works in 1904. Engines like this powered the short passenger trains which stopped daily at Biscayne through the late teens, when larger engines took over.

12TH STREET FROM AVENUE D., LOOKING EAST, MIAMI, FLA.

In 1906–07 Miami, with its first electrically powered streetcar, was already a bustling city, having been founded in 1896. Burdine's, Miami's hometown department store, is shown on the right. Kress's is right next to it. This view looks east on 12th Street.

Miami was bustling while Biscayne, though having been the county seat from 1870 until 1880 and being the home of numerous coontie mills and sawmills, was, for the most part, agricultural. It would remain so until Hugh Anderson, Ellen Spears Harris and other developers arrived, bringing grandiose plans to the rural farmland and putting an end to the backwoods nature of the area.

Three
Becoming Miami Shores

Tennessee developer Hugh Anderson, who had previously become a millionaire by building the Venetian Causeway and developing the Venetian Islands was on the verge of his greatest moves, purchasing the pineapple farms from L.T. Cooper and forming the Shoreland Company. Anderson, no small thinker, had grandiose plans for the 2,500 acres (less the land that Cooper kept and which he named "El Portal"), which he planned to call Miami Shores and develop into "America's Riviera."

The Florida land boom of the early twenties began to unfold as servicemen returned from World War I and Carl Fisher's early Miami Beach publicity, with pictures known as "cheesecake," showing beautiful young women in brief bathing suits (not brief like today's, but brief for the times!), flooded Northern newspapers in midwinter. It was a glorious time and the boom developed slowly, beginning in 1920 and reaching flood tide proportions by 1925.

Anderson knew, as did Carl Fisher in Miami Beach and George Merrick in Coral Gables, that he had to have top-notch people associated with him in the efforts to develop the area north of Northeast 87th Street. His lineup of colleagues and associates was every bit the equal of Fisher's and Merrick's. His purchase of what would eventually become Miami Shores stretched from where it shared a common border with El Portal on the south to its western border across 91st Street and then north on Northwest 2nd Avenue.

However, what most do not realize is that the original Shoreland Company property was not contiguous, but rather was separated, with part of it being south and north of today's Northeast 123rd Street, and, in fact, extending north to and above Arch Creek, where Anderson planned to build a $2 million hotel. A causeway, at or near the site of today's Broad Causeway, was planned to connect to Miami Shores Island via the "Grand Concourse" (today's Northeast 123rd Street in North Miami) and then continue to the beach side. The island, as shown on the Shoreland Company map, was planned to be six hundred acres, with the map text stating the island would be almost double the size of all the islands in the lower bay combined.

Anderson had numbered the Venetian Causeway islands as one through four, starting with the first island west of Belle Isle, the closest island to Miami Beach, and the planned mid-bay causeway, shown on the map, shows islands five through nine, all oriented north-south with a bridge connecting island number nine (the farthest north) with the south end of the planned Miami Shores Island.

Most of the land sales for the company were conducted from the offices at 125 East Flagler Street. The street numbering system was changed in 1921, and the current numbers through the north county line reflect the "new" numbering system. There are four quadrants—northeast, southeast, northwest and southwest. Flagler Street (old 12th Street) runs east-west, dividing north and south, while old Avenue D, renamed Miami Avenue, runs north-south and divides east from west.

While Shoreland Company land sales totaled multiple millions of dollars, the events of 1926, related earlier herein, would bring an end to the boom and eventually the demise of the Shoreland Company. During the boom, in 1926 Arch Creek became Miami Shores, but with the Shoreland bankruptcy Bessemer Properties took control of the former Shoreland entity in 1928. In 1931 the state legislature granted a charter creating Miami Shores Village (which had a larger population than the community north of it which had borne that name for six years). On January 2, 1932, Frank O. Pruitt became the first mayor of the new municipality. The former Miami Shores became the town of North Miami and that story is in the first of the North Miami chapters.

Miami Shores today has almost ten thousand residents and a highly respected police force of thirty-six officers and ten civilian employees. It is a stable community, maintained to the highest standards by the fact that the council refuses to grant zoning variances. While several of the surrounding areas have seen serious declines in property values, Miami Shores homes and property continue to increase in value and worth, both for real estate purposes and because the village is a fine place in which to live and raise a family.

45.-

RMS

****

WHAT CENSUS TAKER MAY FIND IN 1930

	1930	1920
Miami	350,000	29,511
Jacksonville	225,000	91,558
Tampa	200,000	51,608
Orlando	75,000	9,282
West Palm Beach	75,000	8,659
St. Petersburg	75,000	14,237
Lakeland	60,000	7,062
Sarasota	50,000	2,149
Bradenton	50,000	3,868
Pensacola	40,000	31,035
Fort Myers	35,000	3,678
Fort Pierce	30,000	2,115
Fort Lauderdale	30,000	2,065
Key West	25,000	18,749
Daytona	25,000	5,445
Okeechobee	25,000	900
St. Augustine	20,000	6,192
Sanford	15,000	5,588
Bartow	15,000	4,203
DeLand	15,000	3,324
Palatka	15,000	5,102
Gainesville	15,000	6,860
Lake City	15,000	3,341
Tallahassee	15,000	5,637
Ocala	12,000	4,914
Sebring	10,000	812
Avon Park	10,000	890
Melbourne	10,000	533
Cocoa	10,000	1,445
Eustis	10,000	1,193

How We May Expect the Leading Cities of Florida to Rank in the Southeast in 1930

	1930	1920
New Orleans	415,000	387,219
Miami	359,000	29,571
Atlanta	300,000	200,616
Birmingham	250,000	178,806
Jacksonville	225,000	91,558
Tampa	200,000	51,608
Memphis	200,000	162,351
Savannah	100,000	83,252

****

MIAMI SHORES

*How large
will
Your Town
be
in Six Years
?*

AMERICA'S MEDITERRANEAN

Anderson wasted no time getting started, and as Merrick (even more so than Fisher) had done, within a short time following the purchase of the land from Cooper, he began to publicize the new "America's Mediterranean." Published in 1924 with projected 1930 census figures for various cities throughout Florida, this very rare brochure lists Miami's population as growing from 29,511 in 1920 to 350,900 in 1930. Size and growth, in those days, were measures of success.

While Coral Gables buses (Fisher did not buy any for Miami Beach) were ubiquitous throughout the eastern half of the United States, Miami Shores buses were rarely seen. This photograph, though from a copy negative, is a rare gem, showing us a Shores bus on the left with a City of Miami bus to the right. It is likely that the Miami Shores bus was used to bring people from Flagler Street north to the Shoreland Company's properties.

Anything "official" relating to the Shoreland Company rates at the highest level of interest in the realm of Miami memorabilia collecting. This letterhead—showing not only the name of the company but also the future name of the municipality—is a true gem. It includes, at left, the names of the company officers. While J.A. Riach, the last name shown, has the title "Publicity," history has not been kind to him. Unlike Steve Hannagan in Miami Beach or Edward E. "Doc" Dammers in Coral Gables, there is little concrete evidence of Riach's work, although it is possible that he produced the Shoreland Company's brochures and booklets.

The idea of a woman in a position of power or influence in the hierarchy of the various developers of Greater Miami was extremely unusual during the boom. The Shoreland Company, however, was proud to boast of a premiere exception: Ellen Spears Harris. Harris took a major role not only in the company but also in the development of the Shoreland properties, and as company vice-president, she was a major force in northeast Dade County history. *Courtesy Warren Bittner collection.*

Like George Merrick, Anderson, Spears and Co. knew that the key to their success was advertising. While Merrick advertised much more heavily nationally, Anderson concentrated on Florida and the South. This marvelous and inviting ad unquestionably draws on both the graphics and layout of the Coral Gables advertising, the "look and feel" of this ad in *Suniland* magazine, circa 1926, being very much the same.

Marshalling major forces of both manpower and construction equipment, the Shoreland Company's contractors worked day and night to create the planned paradise that Anderson and Spears envisioned. Because of the parkway it is evident that this is Northeast 96th Street and it is thought by Maria Temkin of the Brockway Library that this view was made at Northeast 4th Avenue. *Courtesy Brockway Memorial Library.*

The homes, like those in the Gables, were built to rigorous standards, both architecturally and materially. This Shoreland Company home, at 107 Northeast 96th Street, like the majority of those built during the boom, has stood the test of time and remains a showpiece of the halcyon days of that era.

Unquestionably it was difficult work preparing the land for the Shoreland Company's development. Though this is an original photo of the blasting that was being done throughout the area, it can be noted that there is a slight blur to the photo, caused by the fact that the shutter of the camera was engaged at the very moment that the dynamite was exploded in May of 1925 at rockpit number one. *Courtesy Warren Bittner collection.*

The blasting would pay off, and the two homes shown on this page are perfect evidence of how Miami Shores was meant to look, and how it would continue to look, as it has aged beautifully through the years. At the top is the home built by Harold M. Wilson, at 339 Northeast 96th Street, between Northeast 3rd and 4th Avenues, while the bottom picture, at 121 Northeast 100th Street, was the residence of Sidney M. Weise. *Courtesy Warren Bittner collection.*

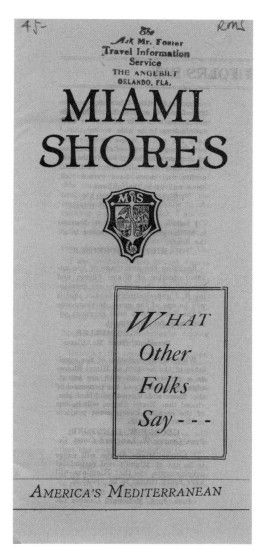

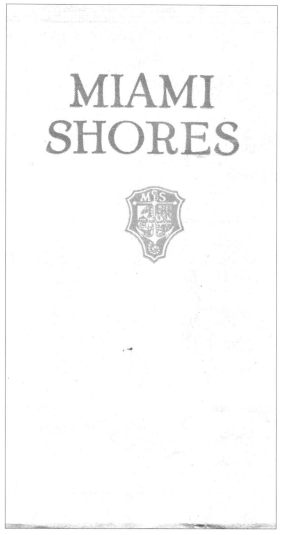

Left: Another of the Shoreland brochures was this piece issued early in 1925, containing quotes praising Miami real estate in general and the Shoreland properties in particular. Among the quoted are bank and hotel presidents—Frank Stoneman, editor of the *Miami Herald* and father of the savior of the Everglades, author Marjory Stoneman Douglas—as well as Roddy Burdine, president of the famous department store, and Ev Sewell, president of the chamber of commerce and a longtime Miami mayor.

Right: With land sales increasing daily and money pouring in, the company issued this stunning twenty-eight-page booklet extolling the glories of Miami Shores, the highlight of which is a full three-page foldout with a map of the Shoreland Company properties and the proposed improvements that were "in the works."

Few things can illustrate better what the developers were up against in terms of preparing the land for homes and roads as this incredible July 1925 view taken from what is approximately today's Northeast 122nd Street looking east across Biscayne Bay. While the company did begin some rudimentary filling, the Grand Concourse (today's Northeast 123rd Street is not the Grand Concourse that exists in Miami Shores now) and the Miami Shores Causeway (today's Broad Causeway) were never built. The proposed Miami Shores Island would eventually be filled on a smaller scale and is today the exclusive home and golf course community of Indian Creek Village.

Above: Although known in later years as the Mercer Building, for owners Claude and Bill Mercer, this building was originally the Shoreland Arcade. The name of the company is facing the camera. At Northeast 96th Street and 2nd Avenue (to our right and left along the long façade), the arcade and its shops were brutalized, as was much of Greater Miami, by the September 17–18, 1926 hurricane. Although all of the developers attempted to put on a happy face, the hurricane was the culminating 1926 event that would doom the great Florida boom and bring about the bust that would follow, putting most of the developers into bankruptcy.

Opposite above: On rainy July 20, 1926, an unnamed photographer snapped this scene looking west from the intersection of Northeast 4th Avenue, Grand Concourse and 96th Street. The Harold Wilson House, at 339 Northeast 96th Street is on the right, the Ellen Spears Harris House (shown up close, below) is also on the right, half a block to the west. The author's home at 330 Northeast 96th Street, directly across from the Wilson House, would not be built until 1953, some twenty-seven years later.

Opposite below: The great Miami photographer Richard B. Hoit took this striking view of the Harris home probably sometime in late 1925 or early '26. The house, on the northwest corner of Northeast 96th Street (then called Shoreland Boulevard), remains today as a stunning example of Shoreland construction. Its interior has been preserved by the several owners following Mrs. Harris's death. *Courtesy Warren Bittner collection.*

Above: An aerial view in the very early 1930s shows a scene familiar to today's Miami Shores residents: the intersection looking north on Biscayne Boulevard where Northeast 6th Avenue leaves the Boulevard, which curves to the right. To the left of 6th Avenue today is Tropical Chevrolet, with Walgreens and Publix located just north of the V. The FEC Railway, as it has since 1896 and continues to do today, runs through Miami Shores and is crossed by 6th Avenue at top left of the photograph.

Opposite: Even with the bust, people who had money still traveled to south Florida. The Jones family, for many years users of their own private railway cars, would park their cars on the sidings in Miami Shores. James Sr., shown here on the rear step of his heavyweight open-platform, private car, would be followed by his son, James Jr., whose car was parked on the siding, then just north of today's Northeast 96th Street on the west side of the FEC Railway tracks. *Courtesy Brockway Memorial Library.*

Roy McKenzie served as Bessemer Properties's "man on the scene" in Miami Shores, following the company's taking the moribund Shoreland Company's holdings out of bankruptcy on behalf of the S.J. Phipps Estate of New York. McKenzie had purchased much of the Shoreland property and is generally credited with being the principal founder of "the Shores."

The charter for the village appointed five men to the first council, with insurance agent Frank O. Pruitt serving as the first mayor, the first city hall located at 9533 Northeast 2nd Avenue, being moved farther north on the same block, to 9545, in 1937.

Barry University opened in 1940 as Barry College for Women, on its way to becoming today's nationally renowned school. The top view shows the college from the air, Northeast 2nd Avenue directly below the camera, Biscayne Kennel Club in the far center background on July 15, 1951.

Barry University's Administration Building, circa 1946.

Originally opened in 1926, Biscayne Kennel Club, at 320 Northwest 115th Street, was far out in the woods and had a difficult time competing against Hollywood, Miami Beach and Flagler dog tracks, all easier to get to. Over time, Biscayne, with its lovely setting and fine neighborhood, became a favored parimutuel locale, shown here circa 1940.

By the mid-1950s it was obvious that new and upgraded facilities were needed, and track management committed the funds necessary to build a completely new facility, the superstructure in place on July 19, 1956. Sadly, without casino gaming to support the parimutuels, Biscayne became the third horse or dog track to close. The site is now the home of the new Doctors Charter School of Miami Shores.

By December of 1952, Joe Hart (later of Castaways Motel fame) opened his newest Pickin' Chicken restaurant between Northeast 6th Avenue and Biscayne Boulevard. The Boulevard is on the lower right, and 6th Avenue is the straight street, center. The FEC runs from center left to upper right.

This depicts the view north on Northeast 2nd Avenue at the intersection of the beginning of Grand Concourse on November 17, 1958. Though not the Grand Concourse originally planned by Anderson and his associates, today's Grand Concourse is a beautiful and wide boulevard that angles northeast from 2nd to 6th Avenues and is one of the Shores's most desirable residential streets.

As tax revenues grew, the village was able to afford its own fire department. The trucks of two different decades are shown. *Courtesy Brockway Miami Shores Library.*

Eventually, Dade (now Miami-Dade) County would take over most of the smaller municipalities' fire departments and Miami Shores's own department is now but a memory. Regretfully, only one person shown is known—longtime Village Manager Lawton McCall at far left. *Courtesy Brockway Miami Shores Library.*

By the late 1940s, Northeast 2nd Avenue had taken on the look of a busy street, as shown in this view, looking north from just south of 96th Street.

Biscayne Cafeteria, one of the few eateries in the village, at 9900 Northeast 2nd Avenue, drew a disproportionate number of people into the Shores. Now long gone, the building is occupied by the Catholic senior center.

From the time he came home from World War II in 1946 until his retirement in 1978, Officer Bill Chester, who walked the "downtown beat," was much loved by all he served, and his name and the memories of his years of dedication to Miami Shores are fondly remembered.

It was an honor to serve as a Shores reserve police officer, and among those who wore the badge over the years were Jerry Fontanella (top row, third from left), Joe Brown (second from right) and Carl Mintz (far right), who were also Miami Shores firefighters prior to the department being turned over to the county. In the bottom row, left to right, are Jim Jones, Charley Blackstock, Al Swenson, Jerry Infanti and Ralph Oliver.

In a different era, the village used several small Reo-built garbage trucks, which would fit inside today's monstrous trash haulers! This is one of the few known photographs of village work equipment. *Courtesy Brockway Memorial Library.*

Peoples National Bank opened its Miami Shores branch on the northeast corner of Northeast 2nd Avenue and 95th Street in the late 1950s. They would later build a new facility where the parking lot is shown here in this January 29, 1959 photograph looking north from Northeast 94th Street. The bank is on the corner, and the long-gone A&P market is just east of the bank in the same building.

The Koop Family issued their own postcard featuring their house, with the printed caption on the back reading, "From Koop's Coop, Miami Shores, Florida."

Another Shoreland Company home is this beauty on the northeast corner of Northeast 96th Street and 10th Avenue, circa 1994.

Shown on August 6, 1956, the Cities Service station, at 9734, was one of three gas stations on Northeast 2nd Avenue. This station, operated by Chuck Orlandi Jr., whose much beloved father, the late Chuck Sr., ran the Standard Station two blocks south on the corner of Northeast 96th Street and 2nd Avenue for many years, is still in business doing automotive repairs, but no longer pumping gas. Chuck Jr. has developed an area-wide reputation for high quality service and prompt repair work.

Almost everything in this view has changed since when this picture was taken. Now the Presbyterian Church at Northeast 96th Street and 6th Avenue has a totally new chapel and all of the lumberyard and industrial buildings east of the church on West Railroad Avenue (now Park Drive) are long gone. The entire stretch today is a church playground and parking lot with new office buildings farther south. The FEC Railway tracks are directly behind the buildings; East Railroad Avenue (now Club Drive) is just east of the tracks. *Courtesy Stobs Brothers Construction Co.*

Contrary to the silliness spouted by those who should know better but who can't seem to help themselves when it comes to pompous exaggerations, the hotel built by the Shoreland Company at 421 Grand Concourse was never owned, visited and likely never even looked at by Al Brown, also known as Al Capone. Fortunately for the Shores, though, the beautiful building, newly rehabilitated, is still in place. This shows the now–apartment house and condo from Grand Concourse. *Courtesy Pat Duffy, Duffy Realty.*

The beautiful courtyard at 421 Grand Concourse. *Courtesy Pat Duffy, Duffy Realty.*

Since he left the market on Northeast 6th Avenue and 105th Street about nineteen years ago to open his own store at 9722 Northeast 2nd Avenue, Norberto Velez and son Nayo have made Norberto's Deli one of Miami's top sandwich emporiums. A great drop-in spot, enjoyed by anybody who knows good food, the deli has become a gathering place to eat-in, take out or just do some local schmoozing. Innumerable members of the community savor the homemade salads, excellent—and large—sandwiches and Norberto's famous homemade carrot and lemon pound cake desserts.

Like longtime village manager Lawton McCall, Ann Vigneron, who came to Miami Shores as village clerk, eventually became a well-known face in the area. With a warm smile for all, Ann was a favorite with everyone who she served and worked with, and since her retirement village hall has never been quite the same! *Courtesy Brockway Memorial Library.*

The village-owned country club was a wonderful place to enjoy, but, unhappily for village residents and its members, it was endlessly subject to political interference, especially beginning in early 1987, when the late Elly Johnson became village manager and essentially ruined the club while tearing the village asunder. Shown in this circa 1952 photograph at the country club swimming pool are the famous Miami Shores modeling twins, Turalura Lipschitz on the high dive and her sister, Tondalaya, sitting on the one-meter board. The pool is now gone, removed and paved over for club parking.

The old Shores Theater at Northeast 98th Street and 2nd Avenue, was almost destroyed by a local well-meaning but misguided group of pseudo-theater enthusiasts, whose tinkering nearly ruined it. In the late 1980s, they took over the venue, which was no longer used for movies, and played entertainment dilettantes, while having no idea or concept of how the business end actually operated. While still a movie theater, though, the Shores drew a good crowd. As shown here, in September of 1966 Bob Hope was starring in *Boy, Did I Get a Wrong Number!*

Moribund and on the verge of being converted to retail space, the Shores Performing Arts Theater was taken over by longtime philanthropists and legitimate patrons of the arts Stephanie and Toby Ansin. The Ansins instituted a new program and a new concept for the building, renaming it the PlayGround Theater and bringing in fine family entertainment and stage plays, helping to bring new life to downtown Miami Shores.

Built by Stobs Brothers Construction Co., a highly respected and longtime Miami Shores–based firm, the new Village Aquatic Center, located just north of the country club on Biscayne Boulevard, provides a wonderful spot for residents and visitors to enjoy water sports all year round. The center is complete with a children's pool, jacuzzi, family areas and competition pool for swim meets. *Courtesy Robert J. Stobs, Stobs Brothers Construction Co.*

Four

Biscayne Park

$\mathcal{L}$ike several other communities in Miami-Dade County, the history and story of Biscayne Park is essentially the story of one man, Arthur Mertlow Griffing—the founder of that unique, lovely and delightful community. On December 31, 1931, 113 of Griffing Biscayne Park Estates citizens voted to change the name of the community to the Town of Biscayne Park. On June 16, 1933, the state granted a charter changing the name to the Village of Biscayne Park.

Arthur Griffing, who hailed from Norwich, New York, first arrived in Florida in 1903, having accepted the job of manager of the Little River Nursery. He built a large home and then built Griffing Biscayne Park Estates, continuing his love of landscaping by planting the area with shrubs and trees to the extent that Biscayne Park Estates resembled a tropical garden.

Early in 1923, he began advertising land available for sale in the *Miami Daily Metropolis*, later the *Daily News*. To entice buyers Griffing offered them complimentary strawberry shortcake if they would come up and look at his development. The beautifully landscaped community allowed him to ask between $4,000 and $4,500 each for homes in the development—an enormous sum at that time. Griffing eventually upgraded the strawberry shortcake incentive to a box of citrus fruit!

During the Depression, the Works Progress Administration built a log cabin for the village with the Federal Emergency Relief Administration providing the labor for the termite-resistant Dade County pine construction. William Green, a regional administrator for the federal programs and a village resident and councilman, was instrumental in the creation of the building that is today a revered historic landmark, which serves as the village hall and police station. On January 24, 1935, the log cabin was turned over to the village and remains the center of operations for the municipality.

Biscayne Park's boundaries today are the Biscayne River and Griffing Boulevard on the west, Northeast 131st Street on the north, Northeast 11th Avenue on the east and Northeast 107th Street on the south, forming an isosceles triangle with Northeast 6th

Avenue entering the south side of the village at Northeast 113th Street and West Dixie Highway, angling in from the north to cross Griffing Boulevard just above 121st Street.

Under the direction of Mayor John Hornbuckle, Interim Village Manager Frank Spence and a dedicated and caring commission, Biscayne Park is poised to move purposefully into the future and remain a caring, nurturing and welcoming residential enclave.

PROPERTY OFFICES N.E. 114TH STREET
AT COR. N. E. SIXTH AVE. AND GRIFFING BLVD.

TELEPHONES EDGEWATER 1511-R
EDGEWATER 1163-W

EDGEWATER HOMES
BISCAYNE PARK ESTATES
(In Greater Miami)
VILLAGE OF BISCAYNE PARK, FLORIDA

WATER FRONT ESTATES
HOMESTEAD TRACTS
IDEAL BUNGALOW SITES
IN RESTRICTED VILLAGE
MANY PARKS AND PLAYGROUNDS
SHADY BOULEVARDS
LOW TAX RATE
NO BONDED DEBT
GEM OF THE
NORTHEAST SECTION
GATEWAY TO MIAMI
12 MINUTES FROM
FLAGLER STREET VIA
BISCAYNE BOULEVARD

April 30, 1935

Mr. R.B. Strock
North Miami, Fla.

Dear Mr. Strock:

I am enclosing some letters just received from the First Assistant Postmaster General and our good friend, Linton Collins of Washington.

You will also be interested to learn, if you do not already know of it, that Postmaster General Farley has instructed the Miami Postal authorities to make an official survey of this territory and they are including the town of North Miami as well as Biscayne Park. This work is in charge of Mr. McLeland to whom I have furnished several maps, and he informs us that if free mail delivery is established it will not eliminate the North Miami Post Office, as this Post Office will continue as heretofore for the convenience of those who wish to use it and for the sale of money orders, stamps, et cetera.

Personally I wish to again express my appreciation for your efforts along this line as well as the good ladies of the village of Biscayne Park, as this is a splendid piece of work.

Sincerely yours,

Arthur M. Griffing

ARTHUR M. GRIFFING

AMG:v

Copy to
Mr. EARL THOMAS

On April 30, 1935, Mr. Griffing wrote this letter to R.S. Strock in the then town (later city) of North Miami. Like the letter on the next page, anything with original Biscayne Park letterhead or with Griffing's signature is at the pinnacle of Miami memorabilia. *Courtesy Village of Biscayne Park.*

Mail Address: Box 761, Little River Sta., Miami   Telephone 7-1255

Glimpes of the River in Biscayne Park Estates
BISCAYNE PARK, FLORIDA

WATER FRONT ESTATES
HOMESTEAD TRACTS
IDEAL BUNGALOW SITES
  IN RESTRICTED VILLAGE
MANY PARKS AND PLAYGROUNDS
SHADY BOULEVARDS
PERFECT DRAINAGE
LOW TAX RATE
NO BONDED DEBT
GEM OF THE
  NORTHEAST SECTION
GATEWAY TO MIAMI
15 MINUTES FROM
  FLAGLER STREET VIA
  BISCAYNE BOULEVARD

Hon. T. J. Maxey,
2041 N. Miami Avenue,
Miami, Fla.

North Miami, Fla.
April 21, 1938.

Dear Mayor:

     If my information is correct, I believe that
some consideration has been given by the Village Council
for the past two or three years or more to the proposition
of placing an occupational license for the operation of
commercial chicken sheds within the restricted areas, but
so far as I am aware, no action of this kind has been
taken, although I understand that within the past month
or two that an occupational license has been imposed upon
contractors and builders who wish to operate within the
Village limits.

     I am not questioning the right of the Village
to impose such a tax upon builders, but I also believe that
a rather heavy occupational license should be placed against
the operation of the commercial chicken plants.

     One reason I am calling the matter to the
attention of yourself and the other Commissioners at this
time is that a lady by the name of Mrs. W. R. Young, who
is the owner of lot 3 of block 15, and who has owned this
lot for nearly fifteen years, is now trying to sell the
lot to a party who wishes to improve it with a dwelling
house and it is reported to us that her prospect will not
purchase this lot while the chicken plants are being
operated in that vicinity.

     Candidly, I do not believe the chicken sheds
are near enough to lot 3 of Block 15 to seriously affect
the lot as a building site, although as long as they are
continued to operate with the apparent sanction of the
Village Commission, and with no license, the question
naturally arises as to how long this condition may be
continued or even extended.

This letter, written by Mr. Griffing to Mayor T.J. Maxey relative to the operation of commercial chicken sheds being in Biscayne Park, is an interesting and candid three-page missive, but, for the collectors, the letterhead plus the information on the left side above the map provide fascinating reading. The third item down mentions "Ideal Bungalow Sites in Restricted Village," confirming that Biscayne Park was, at the time, "suitably restricted for the protection of homeowners." This meant that those of the Jewish faith—similar to the deed restrictions on a good few lots in Miami Shores—were not welcome at the time. *Courtesy Village of Biscayne Park.*

The Biscayne Apartments, at 11530 Griffing Boulevard, were for many years fashionable residential addresses. Griffing Boulevard, paralleling Biscayne River, is named for the city's founder.

The log cabin is both the village hall and police station. The police department, on the west side of the building, is shown here. *Courtesy Biscayne Park Village.*

As the good people at village hall reported to this writer, "It seemed like Ed Burke was mayor for as long as anybody can remember." Indeed, he was the voice of the village for many years. Here he is shown on board an elephant brought in from the Crandon Park Zoo for the village's fiftieth anniversary celebration in 1983. *Courtesy Biscayne Park Village.*

At the village's sixtieth anniversary, he is shown in a little bit more conventional conveyance than in the previous picture, riding with Commissioner P. Hinck. *Courtesy Biscayne Park Village.*

The late Congressman Bill Lehman was for many years a Biscayne Park resident and was always active in the village's civic affairs. Here, at left, he presents the winner's trophy for the 1974 Miss Biscayne Park contest to contestant Candy Akerman, with first runner-up Annette Anderson to Candy's right, and, next to her second runner-up Kathy Barker. *Courtesy Biscayne Park Village.*

For the village's fiftieth anniversary celebration in 1983, the Civic Club put together a wonderful float commemorating the first fifty years and looking ahead to the next fifty. At the time of publication, incredibly enough, twenty-four of those years have already past. Time, it appears, does fly when we're having fun, and one thing the Biscayne Park folks have always known how to do is have fun! *Courtesy Biscayne Park Village.*

In 1995 or '96 the police department posed for a group photo. In the top row, left to right, are Jeff Kaplan, Mike Leoni, Julio DaSilva, former chief Ron Gotlin, former chief Barry Noe, Sergeant Mike Grandinetti, Joe Fisher, who is currently public works director, Sergeant Mike Marchese and Valentine Benitez. In the bottom row, left to right, are Al Mateos, William Meyers, Tim Morris, Mike Gusman, Sergeant Elizabeth Albert, present Chief Mitchell Glansberg, David Murado and Carlos Mesa. A good few of these men and women remain with the village today. *Courtesy Biscayne Park Village.*

While the year of this photograph is unknown, it is a fine look at the interior of the log cabin village hall, set up for a council meeting, with (from left) Commissioners William Bandrimer and Charles McGaughey, Mayor Ed Burke, Village Clerk Jeanette Horton and Commissioners James A. Reeder and Walter Peterson. The log construction of the building is highly evident in this view, and the building is a designated historic site. *Courtesy Biscayne Park Village.*

Above: Among the beautiful homes in "the Park" was that of Miami industrial buildings developer and owner Ben Pumo, at 12015 Griffing Boulevard. Mr. Pumo's son remains active in the Miami business community today. The photograph was taken January 7, 1955.

Opposite: Elections in Biscayne Park have always been rollicking, interesting and exciting events. When William B. Peterson, a resident for thirty-five years and a member of the commission for twelve, ran for re-election in 1979, he issued this two-sided 3¼-by-5½-inch advertising piece, the back extolling his achievements, availability to the citizenry, and his club, church and organization memberships. *Courtesy Biscayne Park Village.*

RE-ELECT
WALTER B.
PETERSON
YOUR COMMISSIONER

Village of Biscayne Park
December 4, 1979

Five

Arch Creek Becomes Miami Shores—But Not for Long!

*T*he story of North Miami—the machinations of the name changes, the fascinating and quirky people who founded what was originally called Natural Bridge and the sometimes unbelievable events that occurred in the area—would likely fill a good-sized book, but we are limited by the amount of space available, hence the story must be condensed to fit the limitations herein.

The first part of our story begins sometime around 1858, when George Lewis and Robert Fletcher, who had lived relatively close to each other on the Miami River, built a coontie mill at Arch Creek, almost next to the fabled natural bridge (just north of today's Northeast 135th Street about a block west of Biscayne Boulevard). A good few people actually settled nearby, and one of them, William S. Milliken, formerly of Maine, died there and was buried in the vicinity.

Captain John Welsh, who owned the Natural Bridge Grapefruit Company planned to start a town, which he wanted to call Natural Bridge. He bought 160 acres, which, while not including the Natural Bridge, were within walking distance. Welsh even laid out the planned town with ninety-six small lots and several five acre tracts, but his plan disintegrated when he was transferred to Key West. Although he would return a year or two later, he shortly thereafter moved to what would become Miami Beach and became the first—and a very highly successful—real estate salesman for the Lummus brothers, who had bought and were developing a good part of what would become one of the world's most famous resorts.

The original Arch Creek community, which lasted from 1900 to 1926, was founded by the Elmirans. This group, from the southern tier of New York state and led by Fred C. Miller, first arrived in 1900. The following year, Miller brought a boxcar full of furniture and equipment and built a home on the approximately one-hundred-acre tract that he had purchased from either Captain Welsh or Charles J. Ihle, who also owned property near the natural bridge. Miller named the land Elmira Farms, which was part of the Arch Creek community, a name that was in the public domain at least by 1893, when the Lantana to Lemon City stagecoach made its last southbound rest stop at Arch Creek prior to continuing on to the Lemon City terminal.

On February 5, 1926, thirty-eight of forty-seven registered voters of the area then known as Arch Creek, with the encouragement of Earl Irons and Arthur Griffing, and with a good bit of the land owned by the Shoreland Company, took the name Miami Shores and became a corporate entity. The new town of Miami Shores actually included Sunny Isles Beach and today's Haulover Park, Bal Harbour and Surfside. The incorporation also included seven miles on the beach side, from the north county line to today's Miami Beach north city limits at 87th Terrace. That would last only until 1931, when state legislator Dan Chappelle, living in what would become the village of Miami Shores, convinced his colleagues to charter the present Miami Shores as the legal state-sanctioned municipality. The community known as Natural Bridge, Arch Creek and then Miami Shores in the area between today's Northeast 125th and 135th Streets would shortly cease to exist, to be replaced in 1931 by the town of North Miami.

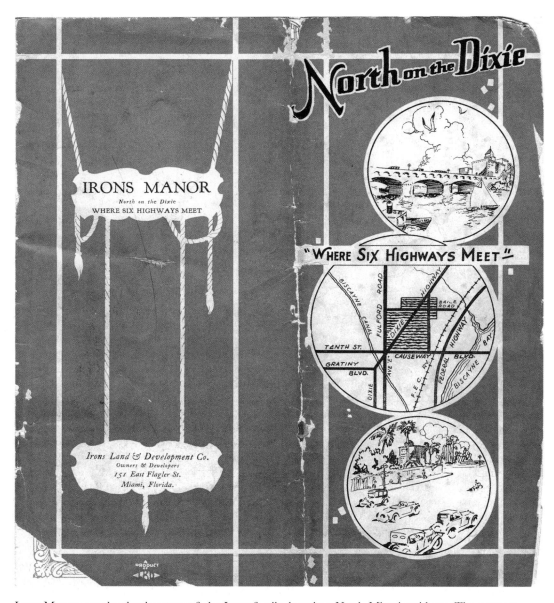

Irons Manor was the development of the Irons family, longtime North Miami residents. The property bordered today's Northeast 125th Street (then called 10th Street and Causeway Boulevard) on the south, Northeast 6th Avenue (then Fulford Road) on the west, approximately 135th Street on the north and Northeast 14th Avenue on the east. As with the early days of Griffing's Biscayne Park Estates, this brochure specifically states that "permanent restrictions have been provided to prevent the possibility of undesirable intrusion," which meant that no persons of the Jewish faith would be permitted to purchase land within Irons Manor. *Courtesy Blair Connor.*

In the beginning of the pioneer era, life and activity centered on a very small area of today's North Miami called Natural Bridge. The area has thankfully been preserved as a county park.

Though the bridge was blown up by developers attempting to stop the sale of the land in the very late 1970s, it was restored and is now the centerpiece of historic North Miami.

Pueblo Feliz—the joyful city—opened January 18, 1926, on Northeast 125th Street and East Dixie Highway (today's (approximately) Northeast 16th Avenue). The opening night event was a spectacular called "Fountania" and Dr. Thelma Peters, as a young girl, was fortunate enough to see the performance.

Severely damaged by the September 17–18, 1926 hurricane, a fire some time later destroyed whatever was left of Pueblo Feliz. The ruins were eventually cleared and the Senator Gwen Margolis community center occupies much of the former entertainment complex today. These images illustrate the unique beauty of the pueblo as well as the glamorized appearance of the entire facility, which was not as large as it was made to appear!

Besides the Gribbles and the other pioneers, some of the earliest settlers in Arch Creek were the Riddle family, and through the courtesy of Bill Riddle, the family's home, with his mother, Thelma, sitting on the porch, is shown here.

On June 29, 1926, a *Miami Herald* photographer by the name of Edwards (first name unknown) took this marvelous photograph of the Irons Manor field office on today's West Dixie Highway in the town of Miami Shores, the name that would be used for today's North Miami until 1931.

This is the original Arch Creek Elementary School, and the photo was taken on the same day as the Irons Manor office shown on the previous page. The elementary school burned down and was supplanted by William Jennings Bryan School, which was both a junior high school and an elementary school.

In this incredibly rare view, made in the late 1920s, the North Miami grade school is shown with "nothing" on the lots across the street. Today's William Jennings Bryan Elementary School is between Northeast 13th and Northeast 14th Avenues facing Northeast 125th Street.

The Potts Building was on the south side of Northeast 125th Street and housed Biscayne Park Hardware and F.B. Potts Cash and Carry store. This photograph was taken sometime in 1926.

TOWN OF NORTH MIAMI
INCORPORATED FEBRUARY 5, 1926
NORTH MIAMI, FLORIDA

_____DEPARTMENT

Above: After the residents of the former town of Miami Shores recovered from the shock of the Phipps interests as well as Bessemer Properties' direction of legislation to give the area south of them the name "Miami Shores," they became the town of North Miami. However, the town stationery, as seen here, continued to carry the original 1926 incorporation date, rather than the date that North Miami came into existence as a separate municipality.

Opposite above: The Bussey Block housed the offices of R.E. Bussey, the realtor who handled much of the selling of Griffing's Biscayne Park Estates. The store on the right was the Biscayne Park Variety Store. Even with the Biscayne Park affiliation, however, the building was in the town of Miami Shores, likely located on Northeast 125th Street.

Opposite below: Miami Shores Frame and Sash Company's building was another of the Edwards photographs made on June 29, 1926. While the location of the building has been lost in the mists of time, the fact that the photograph is extant testifies to the existence of the company.

Six

And Then…North Miami!

*A*s a result of the 1926 hurricane, plans were cancelled for a causeway to deliver municipal services to the beachfront area. The residents of Sunny Isles Beach were receiving nothing in return for their taxes and that "nothing" included the lack of water, police or fire protection, garbage pickup and every other function normally associated with a municipality. It was due to that lack of service that the beach area instituted a lengthy lawsuit to separate from the town of Miami Shores and simply become an unincorporated community within Dade County, a situation which would remain until incorporation as Sunny Isles Beach in 1997. (For the complete history of Sunny Isles Beach, the reader is directed to *From Sandbar to Sophistication: The Story of Sunny Isles Beach*, also published by The History Press.)

Finally, by order of a 1931 Florida Supreme Court decision, the seven miles of Atlantic oceanfront property from the Broward County line southward to Surfside were removed from the North Miami town limits. The wealthy Bessemer Properties, on behalf of the Phipps interests, lobbied the 1931 Florida Legislature to grant their former Shoreland Company holdings south of what was the Town of Miami Shores the name "Village of Miami Shores," and the legislature did so. It also passed an official act abolishing "Town of Miami Shores" as a name, thereby requiring the local population to choose a new name. The abolished Town of Miami Shores was renamed the Town of North Miami. In 1933 Cecille Sevier and Ella S. Klefeker became the first two women elected to the town council. The 1940 census stated that 1,973 inhabitants lived in the Town of North Miami.

At the end of World War II in 1945, a large and constant influx of former military veterans and their young families changed the face of North Miami by ushering in a great period of growth. Homebuilding, roadbuilding, shops, stores, office and business construction then continued for the next several decades almost nonstop. By 1951 it was reported that North Miami was one of the fastest growing towns in the United States, and in 1952 the town voted to adopt a new charter and a new name. The new charter, enacted as an official statute by the Florida Legislature on May 27, 1953, provided for the establishment of a full-time administrative head (city manager form of government) to carry out the policies of the elected mayor and city council, thereby allowing the former town to become today's nationally recognized City of North Miami. The city is now home to the Museum of Contemporary Art, an active, dedicated and highly committed Chamber of Commerce, numerous fine restaurants, North Miami High School and several middle and elementary schools fed by upscale neighborhoods, such as Sans Souci, Keystone Point and the vibrant and active West Side communities.

The city is also fortunate to have a superior municipal library, an active and highly utilized parks and recreation department and a nationally accredited police department. The Carl Mertes Arch Creek Park and Preserve, named after a North Miami police officer killed in the line of duty and maintained by the Arch Creek Historic Trust, contains the rebuilt natural bridge and along with the Elaine Gordon (beloved longtime state legislator) Enchanted Forest Park, within which is a pony track for children, are two of the parklands that an interested, caring and involved citizenry were able to preserve for the future.

Additionally, the Oleta River State Park, Florida's largest urban area state park is part of the city. Perhaps most importantly, the Biscayne Bay Campus of Florida International University, the state university in Miami and home to the university's Schools of Marine Sciences, Journalism and Hospitality Management, is located in North Miami. North Miami's slogan, "City of Progress" is an apt sobriquet for this vibrant, youthful and always exciting city.

MIAMI
COUNTRY DAY
AND RESIDENT
SCHOOL FOR BOYS.

Miami Country Day School, at 601 Northeast 107th Street, is in the unincorporated area just north of Miami Shores and with the growth over the last several years has become one of the largest private college prep schools in south Florida. This is their circa 1957 descriptive booklet and promotional piece.

Now long gone, Southern Palm Motel, at 1298 Northeast 111th Street was one block west of Biscayne and was a lovely pre–air conditioning winter stopping place for those not going to downtown Miami or Miami Beach.

This is the intersection of Northeast 11th Avenue and 111th Street on November 19, 1953. The area today looks quite a bit different then it did over fifty years ago!

Totem Apartments were east of Biscayne Boulevard, at 1580 Northeast 111th Street. This circa 1952–54 postcard shows the style popular at the time, with single-story motels and a grassy patio and sitting area between the two buildings.

Mur-Will Bayview School was at 1650 Northeast 111th Street. Shown on December 18, 1956, the sign for the school is visible between the two doors, hanging from the eaves of what was quite obviously originally nothing more than a duplex.

Four Palms Motel was at 1567 Northeast 116th Street, one hundred yards west of Biscayne Boulevard. None of the motels in the unincorporated area within Miami Shores and Biscayne Park and North Miami is still in use as originally built, and they have all, if they remain extant, become rental housing.

An aerial view of northeast Dade County taken on May 23, 1956, is nothing short of fascinating, with what would become Sans Souci, east of Biscayne Boulevard mostly filled in at center. To the left is the Broad Causeway and left of the causeway is Keystone Point, no longer with any thought of being a fly-in community centered around a private plane landing strip.

A closer look at the area more widely shown above, taken on September 30, 1956, has us looking directly down at what would become the Cricket Club, as well as Sans Souci to the left. The area shown includes the long-gone and mostly forgotten Biscayne Boulevard Drive-In Theater at 11491 Biscayne Boulevard. The streets running from left to right in the photograph are (closer to camera) Northeast 16th Avenue and just beyond that, Biscayne Boulevard, the point at which 16th Avenue merges into Biscayne is at right.

A unique look at both Keystone Point and Sans Souci—in the distance—shows us both North Miami developments in process on November 19, 1953.

Keystone Point, partially developed, circa 1955–56. The road at bottom is Northeast 123rd Street.

This incredible view shows the beloved hall of the town of Miami Shores circa 1930—before it became the town and later city of North Miami. This building was torn down, much to the distress of North Miami historians, and replaced with a modern version, which provides much more space, but has many structural problems and has created great distress for succeeding city administrations.

With North Miami still a town, citizens lined up in front of town hall to cast their ballots in the 1948 presidential election.

This view, made prior to 1935, shows the residence of Mr. and Mrs. W.W. Marmaduke. While it is a beautiful home, the address is not shown, hence difficult to identify location today.

The town was able to manage and operate its own water plant for its citizens. It was built at 12340 Northeast 8th Avenue and was still in operation fifty-six years after opening.

For many years, Edward Taigman was associated with North Miami politics and was also a property owner. His Taigman Building—on the northwest corner of Northeast 6th Avenue and 125th Street, although replaced by a new Walgreens several years ago—is well-remembered by longtime North Miamians.

One of North Miami's longest serving employees, E. May Avril was city clerk almost for longer than anyone could remember! Shown here on January 20, 1959, May's tenure lasted for several decades. If anybody in North Miami knew which closets the skeletons were in, it was May!

On the site of today's North Miami Library and National Guard Armory once resided the North Miami Zoo, and just the mention of that wonderful and happy place brings back joyous memories to the adults who once visited when they were children. Having moved from Opa-Locka, the zoo was not only the home of specimens such as the giant Galapagos tortoises but also housed, for some years, Captain Roman Proske's Tiger Farm.

Prior to the zoo's closing Captain Proske is shown here with one of his tiger cubs. The captain later moved the tiger farm to Biscayne Boulevard where it remained until the mid-1950s.

For many years, from the early 1950s until, if memory serves today's North Miami historians correctly, the mid-1980s, Ernie Skog operated Ernie's Camera and Photo Shop at 583 Northeast 125th Street. Ernie, shown here behind the counter, is happily assisting a beautiful young customer. (Lucky Ernie!)

But Ernie did more than operate the shop and was active in civic affairs including the Boy Scouts, participating as a scoutmaster in the chartering of North Miami Boy Scout Post 9 on January 26, 1955. Ernie is third from left in this photo.

Sometime in the mid-1960s (probably about 1963–64) North Miami's fine fire department opened its Station Three on Northeast 8th Avenue, across from the library, on the former site of the zoo. Taken over by the county in the early 1980s, the station's trucks were moved to Northeast 16th Avenue, and the building is now used for other purposes.

In 1967 the fire department celebrated its 100 percent participation in the United Way, a number of the proud employees of the department shown posing on truck 201.

Though now a music store at 13630 West Dixie Highway, this building began life as the Popiel School and North Dade Jewish Center. Eventually, the congregation would move north, and after several mergers, it is now located north of Ives Dairy Road on Northeast 26th Avenue. This view was made on April 4, 1954, shortly after the temple opened.

Though the temple was but a block south, the Blue Royal Motel, at 13750 West Dixie, advertised itself as "catering to a restricted clientele," meaning Jews were not welcome. The Blue Royal remains today as an apartment motel and a local bar, catering to all who wish to enjoy its facilities!

The Taigman Building is shown here in all its glory! This photograph, made on August 17, 1953, looking at the building from the south side of Northeast 125th Street, shows, among other stores, Chapman's Pharmacy, Ernie's Photo Shop, Richard's Jeweler, North Miami Package Store and Jack's Cycle Shop.

On October 24, 1956, the camera was trained on the corner of Northeast 6th Avenue, West Dixie Highway and 125th Street, looking east from in front of the Taigman Building. The Standard station across the street is now Chevron and in the distance we can see Joe's Toggery and the North Miami water tower. Things have changed somewhat since then!

Banks were a great part of a growing North Miami, and on March 27, 1951, a local group of financiers opened a storefront American National Bank. With the growth of the city the beautiful building shown here opened on Northeast 125th Street on January 24, 1955. Going through several changes of bank names and ownerships it is today a branch of Bank of America.

The North Dade National Bank, at 12326 West Dixie Highway attracted the younger set with its Hopalong Cassidy Savings Club. November 10, 1951 was Hopalong Cassidy Savings Club Day, which, with its promotions, attracted many members, here lined up at the teller's window.

On September 28, 1956, the photographer was positioned in the middle of Northeast 125th Street looking west from 7th Avenue. Tops Restaurant anchors the northwest corner while the building on the southwest corner, although experiencing a complete change of tenants, remains today exactly as it appears here.

Taken about a year after the previous picture on October 5, 1957, the view is at the same intersection but the camera is looking north on Northeast 7th Avenue. What had been Tops Restaurant has since had a name change to Jack and Jill.

A little fender bender in the street directly in front of the camera gives the viewer a fascinating look at Northeast 126th Street and West Dixie Highway on April 9, 1958. The North Miami Theater (later Miamiway, now closed) is on the right and the building on the left housed a doctor's office.

North Miami police car 182 is on the scene at West Dixie and Northeast 132nd Street on September 10, 1958. The buildings still look the same, but the former Carvel, down the block to the left, is now a fast food restaurant.

12905 Northeast 8th Avenue is still the location of the First Baptist Church of North Miami. Though the photo is undated, it is evident that the church is newly built and that Northeast 8th Avenue is being widened.

Oh, how they loved Marcella's! For years it was the gathering spot for all the kids and families, whether on weekends or after North Miami High games. Shown here in its Northeast 139th Street and West Dixie Highway location on April 19, 1957, the buiding is also occupied by Wright's 5&10 Cent Store and Hamburger Castle at the south end. Notice that there are no buildings on the east side of the street!

North Miami's "west side" centered on the great business street of Northwest 7th Avenue, which was—and is—a street of commercial stores, gas stations, strip shopping centers, fast food restaurants and numerous other enterprises. Paul's Self-Service Drugs was there, as was Jennings 5&10, the latter at 717 Northwest 119th Street. Though there is no date on the "Paul's" photo, the view of Jennings below was made on June 28, 1958.

On September 23, 1957, the Westview Elementary School Baton Group paraded south on Northwest 7th Avenue south of 125th Street. The Bar-B-Q Barn, which has been closed for several years, was on the east side of the avenue.

For many years operated by Jimmy Pace and Randy Spreen, Randy's, at 13420 Northwest 7th Avenue, was one of the West Side's great favorites. Now long gone, it is fondly remembered by those who enjoyed the food and camaraderie there.

Photos of restaurant and bar interiors are rare, no matter the locale, hence it was unquestionably great good fortune to find the several that are featured herein, including Donovan's, at 14670 West Dixie, on April 1, 1954. The Erin Go Bragh banner hung proudly in this Irish pub!

Still a favored spot in North Miami, the American Czechoslovak Social Club, at 13325 Arch Creek Road, remains a happy gathering spot for social get-togethers and other events.

Another of the warmly remembered spots in North Miami was Claire's Fiesta Room and Luncheonette at 12350 Northeast 6th Avenue. Both exterior and interior, the latter showing the smiling staff, are shown circa 1953–54.

For many years the Baglione family owned and operated the Pure station on the south side of Northeast 125th Street, just west of the FEC tracks at 1375. This view was made sometime in 1947 and is from a family collection.

Northeast 125th Street curves east as soon as it crosses the FEC tracks eastbound and emerges from the curve as Northeast 123rd Street. Shown here at 1590 Northeast 123rd Street on July 3, 1957, is another North Miami gathering spot, the Snack Shop, which featured nineteen-cent Texas burgers.

PIERRE'S RESTAURANT - LOUNGE - PATIO
Broad Causeway, off Biscayne Blvd., North Miami, Fla.

Today, just east of Biscayne Boulevard on Northeast 123rd Street, there is a Wendy's fast food restaurant, but that location was the site of, until a fire of suspicious origin destroyed the last of the three great restaurants that had been there, a wonderful dining venue, and Pierre's, shown here, was the first and is the least remembered. Pierre's was followed by one of Greater Miami's most intimate rendezvous, The Court of the Shadows, and, later, by New York's Cattleman Restaurant, the latter two evoking strong memories from longtime Miamians.

Just a block farther east of the restaurants on the same side of Northeast 123rd Street, an Oldsmobile dealership opened in the early 1950s, first known as Potter Olds and then Fincher (after Dick Fincher, the husband of screen star Gloria DeHaven) Olds, finally ending its days in the 1990s as Beach Oldsmobile. The site has been cleared and awaits office or stores redevelopment.

In 1960, with great hoopla and fanfare, and with an honor guard provided by Miami Military Academy (which was located at Northeast 106th Street and Biscayne Boulevard, now the site of the Quayside condominium complex), North Miami General Hospital held its topping-off ceremony. Accompanied by the usual political speeches and a great sigh of relief from the community that local healthcare was available—without having to go to North Dade Medical on Northwest 95th Street, to Miami Beach or way out 167th Street to Cloverleaf Hospital—the hospital was an important part of the northeast Dade community until it closed in the late 1980s.

123

A fine and modern facility when opened, North Miami General simply could not modernize to keep up with changing health needs and regulations and was sorely missed upon its closing. Vacant for some years, it was eventually purchased by a group from Rhode Island, who converted it to a cooking trades school.

This lovely blonde swimsuit model, Mary Robbins, poses on a Keystone Point seawall Today Mary is an accountant.

Souvenir Program Five Cents

1958 - 59 Season

North Miami
Senior High School
Pioneers

1959 Home Schedule

Jan. 16	Stranahan
Jan. 17	Coral Gables
Jan. 23	Hialeah
Jan. 30	West Palm Beach
Jan. 31	Miami Beach
Feb. 5	South Dade
Feb. 7	Curley
Feb. 10	South Broward
Feb. 14	Central Catholic
Feb. 17	Fort Lauderdale
Feb. 21	Jackson
Feb. 29	Edison

We Fill Prescriptions

S & U Drugs
14763 N. E. 6 Ave.

Three Registered Pharmacists
Wilson 7-8697

Bob's Hardware
14755 N. E. 6th. Ave.

SHERWIN WILLIAMS PAINT
Garden Supply Tools
Plumbing & Electrical Supplies

Phone-WI 79741

When You Stop   SERVICE
We Start   As Close As Your
        Phone WI 53321

KING'S CITIES SERVICE
CITIES SERVICE PRODUCTS
Pick-Up and Delivery Service

14970 N.E. SIXTH AVENUE   Mechanic
North Miami, Florida   On Duty

Above left: Beautiful brunette Connie Scott worked at the North Miami Publix shortly after it opened in 1964 or '65. Connie has since become Connie Scott Manley and is one of the family members who operates the well-known longtime Miami jewelry firm, Manley's Jewelers, the store just south of Publix in the same 127th Street Shopping Center where Mary worked more than forty years ago!

Above right: The students of North Miami High, with its green and white colors, have always been the "Pioneers." The football program for the 1958–59 season included games against several Dade and Broward County schools including Coral Gables, Hialeah and arch-rival Miami Beach.

Right: Because Miami Transit buses did not come far enough north to serve most of Dade County beyond the Miami city limits, Coast Cities Coaches, in 1947, began a service that would last until the late 1960s, when the county took over all bus operations from the private companies. This October 20, 1947 schedule shows the service provided to all of the areas included in this volume as well as to areas farther north and west within the county.

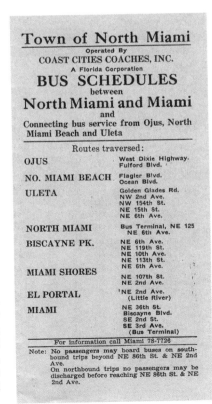

Town of North Miami
Operated By
COAST CITIES COACHES, INC.
A Florida Corporation

BUS SCHEDULES
between
North Miami and Miami
and
Connecting bus service from Ojus, North Miami Beach and Uleta

Routes traversed:

OJUS	West Dixie Highway. Fulford Blvd.
NO. MIAMI BEACH	Flagler Blvd. Ocean Blvd.
ULETA	Golden Glades Rd. NW 2nd Ave. NW 154th St. NE 15th St. NE 6th Ave.
NORTH MIAMI	Bus Terminal, NE 125 NE 6th Ave.
BISCAYNE PK.	NE 6th Ave. NE 119th St. NE 10th Ave. NE 113th St. NE 6th Ave.
MIAMI SHORES	NE 107th St. NE 2nd Ave.
EL PORTAL	NE 2nd Ave. (Little River)
MIAMI	NE 36th St. Biscayne Blvd. SE 2nd Ave. SE 3rd Ave. (Bus Terminal)

For information call Miami 78-7726

Note: No passengers may board buses on southbound trips beyond NE 86th St. & NE 2nd Ave.
On northbound trips no passengers may be discharged before reaching NE 86th St. & NE 2nd Ave.

Wisely recognizing the need for a northeast Miami-Dade County facility, the leadership of Miami's public research university, Florida International, opted to open a large full-service campus on property within the City of North Miami in the area known as the Graves Tract. This land was part of the 1,900 acres purchased by Harvey Baker Graves, the founder of Sunny Isles Beach, which originally extended from today's Northeast 135th Street and Biscayne Boulevard to Northeast 163rd Street and which went east to the Intracoastal Waterway and included today's Sunny Isles Beach. This marvelous view of the campus includes the academic buildings, the aquatic center at near left and at far left, the Kovens Conference Center, a major northeast Miami-Dade meeting and convention facility. In the distance (this view actually looks southwest) are the condominiums of North Miami and northeast Miami-Dade.

Seven

Marching up the Boulevard

While Northwest 7th Avenue, West Dixie Highway and Northeast 123rd and 125th Streets are important commercial and business arteries in North Miami, the main street for all of northeast Miami-Dade County is, unquestionably, the Boulevard.

When locals use that term—"the Boulevard"—it simply goes without question which street is being referenced. Whether in Miami or to the north county line, the Boulevard means Biscayne Boulevard, that great sometimes-as-many-as-eight-lanes highway, which is U.S. 1 in Miami-Dade and which passes through El Portal, Miami Shores and North Miami en route north. Biscayne Park is several blocks west of the Boulevard, but the geographic coverage of this book includes the unincorporated area north of Miami Shores, from Northeast 105th Street to Northeast 121st Street, the southern boundary of North Miami.

Biscayne Boulevard has been the location of motels, restaurants and tourist attractions that have been enjoyed by innumerable residents and tourists since the early 1930s, and while not every single one of them will be commemorated herein, many of those places, from 87th Street north to 151st Street, will be shown.

Simply put, the purpose of this chapter is to bring back great memories, engender good and happy thoughts of a time gone by and, most importantly, put a warm smile on the face of each person enjoying his or her memories of a past that may be gone but that can live on through the pages of this book.

The Merry Go Round was at 8800 Biscayne, now the site of a gas station, and some small stores. For the years it existed, the Merry Go Round featured the largest wooden dance floor in the South.

The Shores Drive In Restaurant was next to the site of the Merry Go Round. When the restaurant was sold in the early 1950s, it became the home of Tropical Chevrolet. The building was essentially unaltered and was easily recognizable, only disappearing when the new Tropical showroom was built in 2003.

The Mount Vernon Motor Lodge was on the east side of the Boulevard at 9300. Part of a several-motel chain, this was the farthest south and is now the site of the Archdiocese of Miami's pastoral center and offices.

For many years, Ollie Trout's Trailer Paradise occupied almost two full blocks from 105th to 107th Streets on the west side of Biscayne. This view looks west, the Miami Shores Canal far left. The property is now occupied by the north side of the Miami Shores Lodge, Busy Bee Car Wash and a large K Mart, with nothing remaining of Trailer Paradise.

The Apache Motel, at 10651, was hot! The lounge was a great meeting and gathering spot for singles. Torn down along with Miami Military Academy in order to provide land for the Quayside Condominium, the Apache is still fondly remembered.

On the west side of Biscayne, at 10760, in the block north of Ollie Trout's was the State Restaurant, one of the few twenty-four-hour eateries in northeast Dade at that time. The building is gone, replaced by an office building and stores.

Rodriguez's Alligator Gift Center, famous for the alligators standing upright on the building façade, was there until at least 1960, possibly a bit later. The building, at 10785 Biscayne, on the east side just south of Clifford's Restaurant (not pictured) is still intact, still looking very much the same, with only a continual turnover of tenants denoting that things are different there.

The Arbordale Lodge was at 10800 and was notable for its uniquely shaped head house, as shown here. Though the motel, on the west side, is gone, most of the structures behind it are still in place.

Miami's old-timers well remember Dolly Madison Ice Cream, but very few knew that the company's plant was at 10800 Biscayne. The plant was in the building that would become the Arbordale Lodge, this picture taken several years earlier than the one above. Another superb Miami photo shows one of the Dolly Madison trucks in downtown Miami next to a Miami trolley car on Southwest First Street, and it is likely that those trucks were loaded with ice cream at the plant shown here.

McCabe Motel was at 10925, east side. Today, as with so many of the other buildings and scenes pictured, nothing of McCabe's remains.

TROPICAL COTTAGES
109th & Biscayne Blvd.—Miami, Fla.

Tropical Cottages was at 10900 Biscayne on the west side and, incredibly, the two-story head house is still in place. Several restaurants were opened and closed in the location, and in 2007 the building was still extant. However, its disrepair is foreboding for the future of this interesting remnant of northeast Miami-Dade history.

While there is now a Dairy Queen on the west side of Biscayne at about 140th Street, just south of the Scorch Restaurant, few remember that the original northeast Dade County DQ was at 10935 Biscayne Boulevard. The store that featured "the cone with the curl on top" is shown at that address on the east side of the Boulevard.

The building that housed the Gloucester House, at 10990, just south of the wonderful La Paloma Restaurant, still exists in 2007. While it is occupied by different tenants, it is certainly recognizable, even though this photograph was taken on January 6, 1957.

Dave Cohen took over a previously terribly mismanaged bagel and deli restaurant, and with patience, hard work, lots of great food and love for his guests, has made Bagels & Co. at 11064, one of the best delis on the Boulevard of Dreams! With great service by Michelle and the waitstaff, and the warmth and attentiveness of Charlie and the busmen, Bagels & Co. has become the place to go for breakfast, lunch or snacks any time one is in the area. *Courtesy Dave Cohen of Bagels & Co.*

Few people remember Howard Preserving Co., but their fruit jelly and preserve labels are big-time Miami collectibles. At Biscayne and 111th Street, few have any memory of its existence.

Shangri-La was another of the almost innumerable Biscayne Boulevard cottage- or cabin-type inns. At 11190, it is so long gone that only the photographs have preserved the memory of it.

The Hi-Hat Club was at 11380 and in this November 29, 1951 photograph it is quite apparent that the assembled group is delighted with whatever it was they were drinking that day.

Joe Clemons's Grandma's Kitchen and Grandpa's Bar is well remembered by the locals. In addition to this location, there were restaurants of the same name on Sunny Isles Beach, on Miami Beach and on Southwest 8th Street in Miami. This view is circa 1951.

With the closing of Grandma's Kitchen on Biscayne, Nohlgren's Painted Horse moved into the same location. Oh how the kids from Miami Beach High (and probably North Miami High) loved that place, famous for its ninety-nine-cent all-you-can-eat dinners! They would bring another entree each time a patron finished one, so it became an eating contest each time the high-schoolers went!

Talk about a moment captured in time! This never-to-be-repeated October 29, 1953 scene is at the intersection of Northeast 16th Avenue and Biscayne Boulevard, looking south. The small building on the left is the gatehouse for the Boulevard Drive-In, which in its day was one of the premiere "make-out" spots for all the kids with cars who lived in the area.

Just north of the point where Northeast 16th Avenue meets Biscayne Boulevard is the building that now houses All-Florida Pools. However, for many years this was the Holiday House Motel at 11720, the structure still today looking very much the same and easily recognizable.

At 11805 Hamilton Realty built their office and sign advertising waterfront lots in Sans Souci—today a beautiful enclave of private homes and apartments—for $10,000. Shown on July 5, 1957, the building was at 11805 Biscayne, which is today the site of a closed Bank of America branch.

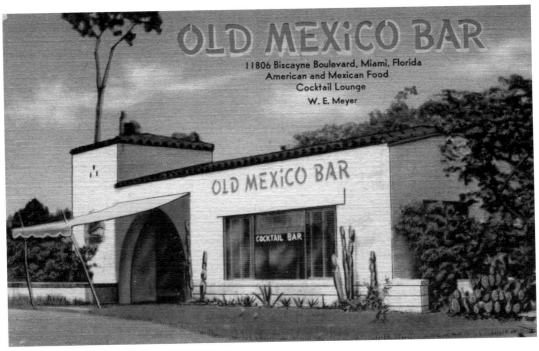

Old Mexico Bar was on the west side at 11806, approximately where Pollo Tropical is today. This unique view is circa 1946.

Looking east over Biscayne on August 17, 1957, the viewer sees Nelson's Trailer Park at 12001 on the east side of the Boulevard. To the right, Sans Souci Boulevard is being graded and the empty land that would be Sans Souci is visible. At far left is Northeast 123rd Street. A Home Depot now occupies the trailer park property with various other stores now on the open land to the left.

There were, happily, "no fleas at Lee's," which was at 11900, just north of the Bamboo Courts and Gift Shop. The building lower left is what would become Old Mexico at 11806. This image is extremely significant not only because it shows Northeast 16th Avenue in the left background but also because Biscayne Boulevard, running from bottom to top at right, is depicted as a tight and narrow four lanes; the photo likely was made sometime in the late 1930s or very early '40s.

Biscayne Villas was another of the cottage-cabin-tourist camp operations. At 121st and Biscayne it has been gone so long that it is difficult to determine which side of the street it was on.

Miami's drivers *never* get any smarter and, in fact, have probably gotten dumber through the years. On December 6, 1956, several of the local geniuses got together in a traffic mishap at Biscayne and 124th Street. We are looking south, and what would become Tyler's Restaurant is under construction on the left side. Going through a number of pygmalions, the building is still intact and today serves as a FedEx-Kinko's print shop and package drop-off store.

Tyler's was open but that didn't stop another several local yokels from having an accident right in front of the restaurant on August 10, 1958. Looking south, the Standard Oil station has recently closed and will soon be replaced with an office building. A bit beyond the gas station a Broad Causeway sign points the way to the then-paradise of Miami Beach via Bay Harbor Islands, Bal Harbour and Surfside.

The North Miami Trailer Park, Inc., on the west side of the Boulevard at 126th Street, billed itself as the most sanitary park in the area with city water and sewer hook-ups to each trailer. To see what would later go on this property, look at the next few pages.

Although the exact year is not available, the Rancher Motel would eventually be built on the property that had been the trailer park at 126th Street. Shown here, circa 1957, is the entrance driveway and the coffee shop.

The Rancher Coffee Shop was a delightful place to eat, and, as will be noted in the March 25, 1958 photograph, the smiling faces behind the counter made it that much more welcoming.

From restaurant to gym, St. Clair's Cafeteria was originally the southernmost anchor of the 127th Street shopping center, with Publix in the middle. After closing the cafeteria, the facility was empty for several years but, happily, was taken over by U.S. 1 Fitness, which is one of the most modern and up-to-date facilities in the state. At 12760 Biscayne, the shopping center includes, among other tenants, Manley's Jewelry and the veterinary clinic of the beloved Dr. Mieke Baks.

Totally enthralled, a large crowd watches one of the Lorow family of Bohemian glass-blowers practice his art in the store at 127th and Biscayne, likely on the east side of the street. Few remember that there was a glass-blower there—just as Anirama, the animated wonderland that held sway for some years at Northeast 123rd Street, has faded from the collective memory. However, the glass-blowers practiced their fine art daily except Monday from 2:00 p.m. until 10:00 p.m., with no admission charged.

It is January 20, 1962, and the photographer happily recorded the existence of the Golden Steer Restaurant at 13005. Although this building is no longer there, the next building north still is, that being the present and longtime location of Woody's steakburgers. For years before, it was the Biscayne Boulevard home of A&W Root Beer.

Weigel's Boulevard Motel was at 13503, that location today the site of a large strip shopping center. On the south end of the center, about where Weigel's used to be, is a Ben and Jerry's among other stores.

Florida Villas Motel was at 13645, on the east side, and at the time this image was made advertised itself as "One of Miami's finest air cooled," which meant "no air conditioning, but we've got fans!"

Above and below: Possibly Atlantic City's best seafood, Hackney's was famous for their lobster and shore dinners. Sometime in the very late 1920s Harry Hackney, the lobster king, opened his first of three stores on Miami Beach. Later, in the late 1940s or very early '50s he moved the operation to 133rd and Biscayne, on the east side of the Boulevard. It really was terrific, but with Harry's decedence, the family closed the restaurant. Like so much else on the Boulevard of Dreams, almost the only memories are in the photographs of another day and another time.

Opening some time in the 1930s, **Hi-Ho Deluxe Cabins**, at 137th Street, was new, modern and clean, but those summer nights without air conditioning must have been murder!

Red Mill Cottages was at 13740 and the family who enjoyed their March stay marked which cottage they were staying in, noting that on that particular March 1953 day, it was 91 degrees.

Flamingo Cottages were on the east side at 13825. As with so many of the other inns, cabins or motor courts of the day, they were not air conditioned.

Chelsea Court, at 13855, published this three-view advertising card, which, while likely an attempt to show different views and angles, managed to make all look the same!

Opposite, above and below: Both locals and visitors enjoyed the Wax Museum at 13899 Biscayne Boulevard. Although replaced by an office building, the mere mention of the Wax Museum brings back happy memories to those who viewed the full-sized dioramas and statues, including the figure of the first name of Florida, Henry Morrison Flagler.

The City of North Miami, in a bold and brave move, purchased a large parcel of land that had been part of the Graves Tract. Harvey Baker Graves, founder of Sunny Isles, now the City of Sunny Isles Beach, bought 1,900 acres from the Flagler System in 1918, and this magnificent wetland was and is part of that purchase. The purpose of the city's buying of the property was to afford it, the county, the state and the nation the opportunity to showcase North Miami and its environs as the home of Interama, the country's

first permanent world's fair. Unfortunately, though the idea was sound and the goal both valid and noble, as with so much else in Florida politics it simply became bogged down in a morass of bureaucracy and political infighting. Eventually the city gave the land to the state with the promise and covenant that it would become Florida's largest urban state park. Now accessed via Northeast 163rd Street and called the Oleta River State Park, the area once meant to be a World's Fair can still be enjoyed by the public.

MIAMI BEACH

HAULOVER BEACH

A rendering of the Interama site as originally proposed shows the Boulevard of Dreams (noted as U.S. Highway 1) to the right, the Sunny Isles (163rd Street) Causeway directly below, Sunny Isles to the left and then, farther south, Haulover Park, Bal Harbour, the Bal Harbor Islands, Indian Creek Village (what had been planned as Miami Shores Island), Surfside and Miami Beach. Florida International University's Biscayne Bay Campus now occupies part of the Graves tract.

THE GREATER NORTH MIAMI
CHAMBER OF COMMERCE

presents

Miss North Miami USA Pageant 2006

MIAMI SHORES COUNTRY CLUB
APRIL 1, 2006

MISS NORTH MIAMI USA is an Official Preliminary to MISS FLORIDA USA,
independently produced by The Greater North Miami Chamber of Commerce

Since 1958 the Greater North Miami Chamber of Commerce has sponsored the Miss North Miami USA pageant. In addition to that gala evening, the chamber hosts, along with numerous other civic events, the Taste of North Miami, and its offices are the meeting site for the Greater North Miami Historical Society. Without Penny, who is director, and Bill Valentine, her wonderful husband, it is unlikely that either organization would be as strong as each is, and in closing the author extends sincere thanks to Penny, Bill and all of the members of the Historical Society for all they do every day in helping to preserve the history of the Boulevard of Dreams.